color
body
feels

A poetic journey

By C. Churchill

c. churchill

*Dedicated to my dreamers,
writers and magic makers.*

What makes a writer? To me writing, like all art, is a form of expression. You will find writing you love and writing you really don't enjoy all that much. Many times, when we set out on a writing journey we may doubt our words. The single most important thing I have found in my writing journey is to write what you know. Some people will love your writings and some people not that much, and that is totally normal. This does not make you an awful writer. This makes you a real writer.

On my journey I found it was a task to keep writing. Some days I wasn't in the mood or didn't have time. Excuses. That is all that was. I decided to challenge myself to write every day.

One helpful tool in doing this was using prompts. Writers block affects us all at one point or another. I was having a few off days and decided to challenge myself by developing a prompt list to keep writing.

c. churchill

Behold! That is where color body feels was born. I figured a one word a day prompt would be plenty simple to follow.

I tried it for a month, then two and then it ended up going for twenty months. And now twelve months or 365 days of writing prompts are here in this collection of poetry.

The poetry I have put in this book is not one prompt per poem but three. In order. Color, body, feels.

Color = a color

Body = a body part

Feels = an emotion

These prompts are meant for practice. The poetry I have included was done in the same manner. You can start anywhere you would like on your journey.

Just start.

I believe everyone has a voice that deserves to be heard.

I hope you enjoy this poetic journey. I know I have.

color body feels

Table of Contents

January   p. 7

February   p. 21

March   p. 35

April   p. 49

May   p. 63

June   p. 77

July   p. 91

August   p. 105

September   p. 119

October   p. 133

November   p. 147

December   p. 161

c. churchill

*Even when you cannot speak,
you can write.*

color body feels

January

c. churchill

January

1. Chocolate
2. Hold
3. Torn
4. Berry
5. Caress
6. Elated
7. Velvet
8. Thrust
9. Forgotten
10. Sterling
11. Sleep
12. Delighted
13. Iceberg
14. Mimic
15. Spoiled
16. Neon
17. Fly
18. Curious
19. Earth
20. Sweat
21. Limitless
22. Dusk
23. Cry
24. Hesitant
25. Sunrise
26. Crown
27. Powerless
28. Coffee
29. Run
30. Open
31. Sorry

color body feels

Does this hold on me

rival chocolate or wine?

I have always loved the finer things

But you I cannot decide

Alas I remain torn

For you come not in a bottle nor a box

Yet your kiss lingers addictive

And I am at a loss

-chocolate, hold, torn

c. churchill

You took a berry
trailed my skin

Left me elated

    In a high
to begin

Caress simple
a longing deep

   A flutter

      A wither

Blush said keep

  Without a worry
without a care

I gave in
to my new flush sin

-berry, caress, elated

color body feels

You covered me in velvet
I was to be your queen

You my king

    Life thrust in

Stole words from my mouth

laid them broken on the table

We found distance in

Our very own happily never
after

-velvet, thrust, forgotten

c. churchill

The sky told a story of
sterling hearts

Ones full of love, delighted

Eyes of shimmer

        hands of gold

Dancing among clouds pure

        as snow

  Visions of sleep and dreams

        a plenty

Until the wind remembered

Reality

-sterling, sleep, delighted

color body feels

Icebergs

Heavy

In lost loves

Echo

We mimic songs spoiled

    Then let go

Where washed away hearts lie

    In waste

                we abide

-iceberg, mimic, echo

c. churchill

Night energy
draws us close

We come ready
curious

Anticipation explodes
neon skies
neon lies

Escape
if just for a moment

In the rhythm of

        the darkness

-neon, fly, curious

color body feels

Falling is limitless

For sweat upon brow

For earth shatters

For beats divine

Crazy fools we are

Reeling in ripped band aids

    and unpacked mistakes

Ready to join loves dance

    again

    Yet we recoil

Licking those wounds

    As if we had never jumped to begin with

-earth, sweat, limitless

c. churchill

I died in dusk
hoping the last cry

        hit echo

Hesitant tears
waited

For a heart no longer, mine

In a hollow corpse
to see if you would return

One last time

      you would take your thumb

            graze my cheek

Wipe my last tear

-dusk, cry, hesitant

color body feels

Feeling only light pressed
naked upon my flesh

The crown I so eagerly waited

Now fallen powerless

To lay in this meadow

Pure washed of regret

Under sunrise and lullaby

  Reborn

    Ready for the next

-sunrise, crown, powerless

c. churchill

Run

    Run

        Run

All we do

Go. Go. Gone

Stop. Coffee. Check.

Stop. Unload. Load.

Stop

                not for me

      not for you

We stop for no one

then we are through

Closed
Open
Closed

Dead.

-coffee, run, open

color body feels

If I collected my sorrys
And I collected my tears

I wonder which would weigh more?

-sorry

c. churchill

color body feels

February

c. churchill

February

1. Coal
2. Laugh
3. Kind
4. Flaxen
5. Blind
6. Lucky
7. Powder
8. Nerves
9. Inquisitive
10. Sangria
11. Voice
12. Bold
13. Rosewood
14. Groin
15. Diminished
16. Heather
17. Torso
18. Desolate
19. Cedar
20. Vein
21. Skeptical
22. Iron
23. Grow
24. Tenacious
25. Parchment
26. Touch
27. Excited
28. Raven

color body feels

My eyes fell dark
no stars to shimmer

No laugh to behold

Coal filled sockets
dancing to a lost tune

Arms around me
they were kind

They tried

But somedays
the smile

Was only there to hide

-coal, laugh, kind

c. churchill

Flaxen beauty

Field of gold

Blind me lucky in kisses untold

Secrets of youth linger in old bones

Creak we do

    slow to move

But hearts have grown

        in skies of wise

And we never reveal what's behind old lies

-flaxen, blind, lucky

color body feels

Powder turned to diamonds

Frigid walk in nerves

Shaky hands

Teary eyes

How did we get this far?

Inquisitive yet knowing

We never really knew

We just fell

As all open hearts do

-powder, nerves, inquisitive

c. churchill

He whispered in my ear
 His voice
    tickling, inviting
Bold words under
      sangria dreams
Toss. Turn
Into me
No holds
   only hearts beating
Fresh
New
Under
 forever sangria skies

-sangria, voice, bold

color body feels

Keeping your heart in a
rosewood box
out of the corner of my eye

Hold for when the warmth of
groin and groan have diminished

I can still see a love turned
to dust

A love we lost in lust

A keeper of hearts I remain

As we play these adult
children's games

In this box

   Out of the corner of my eye

-rosewood, groin, diminished

c. churchill

Walking among the heather

Feeling the brush

Torso to pollen

 In this blush

Winds to my cheek

 Desolate

   But full

I wonder if the heather knows

        I am here

I wonder if anyone knows

        I am gone

-heather, torso, desolate

color body feels

May we wander

Under cedar boughs

Preserving veins

Filling memories

Skeptical of next steps

Forgetful of those who left

May we wander

Under cedar boughs

Protected from the once was

    living in the now

-cedar, view, skeptical

c. churchill

My will is iron

    yet I grow

Tenacious

    some will say

I tend to look toward survival

        because alas

Tomorrow

    is another day

-iron, grow, tenacious

color body feels

I touch this parchment

Not excited

Not with glee

When this ink hits

It hits every nerve

Exploding

The what haves

The what could have beens

Into myriad of whys

Then I sleep

As all the ink dries

-parchment, touch, excited

c. churchill

Midnight memories

Stopped in tracks

Kisses given

Without one back

The raven sees what we do not

Crying moon tears

For our sorry lot

-raven

color body feels

c. churchill

color body feels

March

c. churchill

March

1. Mahogany
2. Breath
3. Feisty
4. Shimmer
5. Dream
6. Bewilder
7. Rainbow
8. Dislocate
9. Strange
10. Steel
11. Curl
12. Crazy
13. Opaque
14. Soul
15. Cursed
16. Shamrock
17. Collar
18. Smitten
19. Marble
20. Focus
21. Taken
22. Turquoise
23. Tattoo
24. Tease
25. Noir
26. Listen
27. Shallow
28. Fog
29. Beat
30. Caged
31. Espresso

color body feels

I caught my breath

Upon mahogany bedposts

Linens on fire

The house in flames

Feisty

Burning

Desire

I lost my breath

In you

-mahogany, breath, feisty

c. churchill

Springs
　　they shimmer
Flow away
　　dreams floating
In ecstasy
On bewildered currents
　　　we shall rise

Over all these moons
Through all these tides

-shimmer, dream, bewilder

color body feels

He washed over me

In rainbows

Strange colors to see

Dislocate this heart

From mind

    Unfold ours

        from mine

As we turn

Eyes closed

Loving eternally

        blind

-rainbow, dislocate, strange

c. churchill

Those steel gray eyes

Directly see

These corners hidden

From normalcy

The places I breathe

The places I am free

He lets me

be me

Even in my crazy

Those steel gray eyes

    have captured me

As if they could murder

    in one fleeting glance

They let my toes curl

        and take this chance

-steel, curl, crazy

color body feels

Opaque she was

And rightly so

Cursed in life

pure in soul

Honey she was

Muddy and sweet

Attracting the swarm

reigning as queen

Opaque she was

And rightly so

Of birds and bees

she had no foe

-opaque, soul, cursed

c. churchill

She left kisses on collars

Smitten boys did dance

Pulling Shamrocks and clover

Hoping for their chance

But this wee lass

Fiery as they come

Left them in tears

Hanging on breadcrumbs

-shamrock, collar, smitten

color body feels

Run your hands
 down marble spaces

Feeling cool touch
 turn warm grazes

Focus on flinched surprise

   singing louder as
temperatures rise

Have you taken the path to
euphoria?

Get on track

Get focus back

Let this song sing of two

Not of one

Not of you

-marble, focus, taken

c. churchill

Maybe these tears were inked just right

Maybe the sky knew

When turquoise dreams teased the night

Scars bled anew

Blood to paper

Ink to skin

Your battles

Tattoo

    your heart within

-turquoise, tattoo, tease

color body feels

tick.

tock.

Listen.

Black the sky

Black my soul

Tick tock.

Listen.

Noir falls behind said eyes

Shallow breaths

Tick.

Tock.

Listen.

Where there is nothing

Where there is empty

Find a pulse

Tick. Tock. Listen.

-noir, listen, shallow

c. churchill

Welcome the fog

In broken places

Welcome the surrounding

In vacant spaces

Why not release this caged heart?

Soothe those cracks

Those beautiful torn fragments

Let yourself be covered

Let yourself be held

Maybe the beat will return to flutter

Maybe the cage will turn to wings

-fog, beat, caged

color body feels

Morning wafts

Sunlight spark

Toss and turn a bit

Smells of love

And espresso

Churn

My heart into this

His love holds me

On fresh melody

Good mornings in sync

Just short of parody

-espresso

c. churchill

color body feels

April

c. churchill

April

1. Ruby
2. Lips
3. Rage
4. Lavender
5. Eyes
6. Peaceful
7. Marigold
8. Feet
9. Lust
10. Indigo
11. Heart
12. Sorrow
13. Rust
14. Spine
15. Fearless
16. Amethyst
17. Shoulder
18. Euphoric
19. Champagne
20. Mouth
21. Burdened
22. Chrome
23. Hips
24. Spirited
25. Crimson
26. Blood
27. Withdrawn
28. Gold
29. Hands
30. Complete

color body feels

These ruby lips
  contain the fire
As rage trapped tongues
Burn high
  then higher
I cannot speak
  of what will become
For my passion rules
Unbridled
Unsung

-ruby, lips, rage

c. churchill

Wash my eyes of lavender

Coat those glares peaceful

Clean the dirt from the glances

So that we fear no evil

-lavender, peaceful, eyes

color body feels

Feet trapped in longing

Among the marigold streams

Light and tender

Not escaping me

A lust filled carpet

We lie awake

Your hand

   to my lip

The quiver

      to the shake

-marigold, feet, lust

c. churchill

I paint indigo lines

Up these frail arms

Tracing blood path

From present to past

My heart rests in red

But spills

  the hue of sorrow

-indigo, heart, sorrow

color body feels

Your pen has rusted
 writing my name
In tears
  your spine has folded
The once fearless gaze
 we held in kind
Now lost
 In
   words
     unloaded

-rust, spine, fearless

c. churchill

The rains kept coming

Although the sun tried to speak

Amethyst petals fallen

Shoulders soaked in meek

Euphoric pleasures find home

Still the ringing in my ears

Calming the storm

Releasing my fears

-amethyst, shoulder, euphoric

color body feels

I swish you in

And swallow you whole

A champagne kiss

From mouth to soul

No longer burdened to hold my breath

Here to savor

Life at its best

-champagne, mouth, burdened

c. churchill

Behind chrome shades

Cool he hides

A saunter

A salsa

A spirited light

Her hips move gently

Cursing all who enter

the fifty shades of hell

She brings to center

-chrome, hips, spirited

color body feels

Fool he was

In his dark realm

  Withdrawn

    Within

Crimson curtains

Blood filled eyes

Laid his bed

No hope

  just lies

-crimson, blood, withdrawn

c. churchill

The sand blazing hot
My hands start digging
Finding solace in depth
Now they are hidden

As the sun
Kissed skin gold
My eyes burned
Setting free
tears in the wind

I was complete
Saturated in solitude

For sin may have my number
But I have forgotten his

-gold, hands, complete

color body feels

c. churchill

color body feels

May

c. churchill

May

1. Violet
2. Eyelashes
3. Doubt
4. Amber
5. Adams apple
6. Envy
7. Aqua
8. Back
9. Grief
10. Azure
11. Breast
12. Guilt
13. Jade
14. Cheek
15. Hope
16. Blush
17. Ear lobe
18. Pleasure
19. Brass
20. Knee
21. Regret
22. Copper
23. Iris
24. Sympathy
25. Charcoal
26. Hair
27. Shame
28. Coral
29. Fingers
30. Ecstasy
31. Ebony

color body feels

Eyelashes hid her smile

As magic fell to earth

In violet gardens

   she stole the sky

Water remains heavy

    on his brow she sat

He may have feared the rain

But there was no doubt

 In these gardens

    His heart remained

-violet, eyelashes, doubt

c. churchill

Adams apple falls far from the
tree of envy

We no longer accept this amber
covered lie

Fossilized truths have lost
their chance

For a brave new world

Will break this sky

And every ceiling before it

-amber, Adams apple, envy

color body feels

Arch your back

Across my table

Let me feel your grief

Give in to the aqua tides

That you so readily seek

-aqua, back, grief

c. churchill

Do you hold that guilt?

Close to your breast

Where you met her

Under an azure sky

Still claiming my heart

-azure, breast, guilt

color body feels

Jade eyes linger

Fingers trail

On hair curled round

On skin so frail

As hope touches my cheek

As my heart screams

Fingers trail

Jade eyes linger

-jade, cheek, linger

c. churchill

I never saw you coming

But you could see my blush

Chin to ear lobe

A dance of insecurity

Or was is pleasure?

Whatever the case

It could be seen from a mile away

-blush, earlobe, pleasure

color body feels

Regret stole the ring
The one you held open for me
The one you cried upon
Telling last wishes and lies

Begging for your truth
Right before I raised my knee
A plain as sight discovery

The brass balls you carry
Began to shudder
Watching your world
Sink under

-brass, knee, regret

c. churchill

I played a song

On the wind

with copper hands

Diluted love

for what was

As an iris held a smile

but the sympathy

Was greater than the desire

-copper, iris, sympathy

color body feels

Shame on you for holding her under the light

Her charcoal eyes not knowing

What was love

What was spite

As she coddles tears of yesterday

You smile

Knowing the game you play

She retreats

Saving love

For another day

-charcoal, shame, smile

c. churchill

Entwine your mind

My sweet love waits

On beaches linger coral

Living last breaths

Before their time

Do they know fear before death?

Or do they only know the
ecstasy of the sky

-coral, fingers, ecstasy

color body feels

If only the night would sing like the day

If only his smile didn't move the tide

Like ebony sheets draped upon my eyes

He hides his intention

And I am always the last to know

-ebony

c. churchill

color body feels

June

c. churchill

June

1. Alabaster
2. Navel
3. Joy
4. Cherry
5. Thumb
6. Sinful
7. Grey
8. Thigh
9. Surprised
10. Burgundy
11. Elbow
12. Inspired
13. Denim
14. Stomach
15. Brave
16. Emerald
17. Booty
18. Unique
19. Lilac
20. Heel
21. Free
22. Lime
23. Tongue
24. Impulsive
25. Honey
26. Rib
27. Alone
28. Peach
29. Jaw
30. Tender

color body feels

Statuesque alabaster skin
 A chill of decades
    burning fire within

The butterflies have
    clamored for joy
Will this day let them soar?

My navel begged to begin
 As their wings
    traveled up my sin

-alabaster, naval, joy

c. churchill

Sweet as lucid pie

Dark cherry thumbs

    Licked dry

Sinful dessert

For pleasure sought

Give me a nickel

For your thought

For desert

   has already filled this table

Enjoy while you

    are still able

-cherry, thumb, sinful

color body feels

Skies of grey loomed out the window East

From the North I saw the sun

It was located just above your thigh

One touch melting

Anticipated

Never surprised

-grey, thigh, surprised

c. churchill

I rest my elbow on burgundy sheets

Swimming in eyes of promise

Inspired by a sleepless night

Feeling it all

Your residue

My wake

-burgundy, elbow, inspired

color body feels

I thought I was brave till your
hand found my sweetness

Where denim met my stomach

Where plans could be foiled

You brought skill

 And I

  as always

Was ill prepared

-denim, stomach, brave

c. churchill

I will always love the pirate
searching my emerald eyes

Finding the booty lacks no
surprise

Unique as the sun flowing under
the moon

My love waits to be your
plunder

Don't come too soon

-emerald, booty, unique

color body feels

I kick my heels
 High to the winds
  For summer brings
Sweet lilac again
Soothing a cold winters cage
 The warmth finally
   Reaches this place
Breaking free
As we all do
After's winters kiss
Is finally through

-lilac, heel, free

c. churchill

Quips and queries round the room

A bar maid swoons

 as your tongue carries

Limes and licks

Impulsive night tricks

Wet and sweet

Her eyes are caught

She stumbles a tray upon the floor

You know your gift

They all want more

-lime, tongue, impulsive

color body feels

They say the rib holds the heart

But what of the honey

Dripping sweet

It fills my body

As if there are no hollows

Even in the night

I am not alone

For the sweetness

Keeps me high

-honey, rib, alone

c. churchill

Hands that hold hearts

    that bleed

Fortunes told

    in a time of need

Your jaw set firm for nothing but lust

A peach filled mouth

A tender rub

You were summer

Blazing hot

She was caught between seasons

-peach, jaw, tender

color body feels

c. churchill

color body feels

July

c. churchill

July

1. Pearl
2. Waist
3. Cold
4. Rose
5. Face
6. Aching
7. Sage
8. Wrist
9. Amazed
10. Ocean
11. Muscle
12. Crushed
13. Opal
14. Loin
15. Devoted
16. Raspberry
17. Palm
18. Empty
19. Midnight
20. Ankle
21. Timid
22. Mint
23. Nape
24. Engrossed
25. Pewter
26. Skull
27. Terror
28. Maroon
29. Skin
30. Passionate
31. Tan

color body feels

Pearls of wisdom

Drop cold onto unheard hearts

As the world we love falls apart

Your hand my waist a thing of the past

Leaving it all

Loves daunting task

-pearl, waist, cold

c. churchill

The aching filled my hearts
despair

With a rose less thorns I saw
you there

My face felt the chill of
longings embrace

You filled my scope

before I could escape

-rose, face, aching

color body feels

You grabbed these wrists

Bound in past

Freed them

Kissed them in sage thoughts

Never amazed with my tremble

You took your calm

Infused it in my soul

Held me close

Showed me my tomorrow

-sage, wrist, amazed

c. churchill

Shells of torment
 crushed beneath
We gave it all
 under full speed
Landing hard
 on an ocean squall
Our muscles
 could no longer hold this fall

-ocean, muscle, crushed

color body feels

I found an opal
 inscribed to us
Saying devoted
 before lost touch
For all the heat
 we made in loin
Our legacy dropped
 before the storm

-opal, loin, devoted

c. churchill

My hands stained
red of raspberry ink

Palms solid
in sweet lust reek

They lay open and empty
Ready to be filled

For summers juices
Are never stilled

-raspberry, palm, empty

color body feels

When midnight called

I took its hand

Fierce sold me

Before timid could speak

Chains you had ankle ready

Were just a shallow attempt

  to keep me weak

-midnight, ankle, timid

c. churchill

Your neck trailed in mint and rye

The nape I held was less than dry

You told me of love engrossed in song

But my dear you were just a drink loved wrong

-mint, nape, engrossed

color body feels

As pewter hands
　stole my voice
You ripped my skull
　from its hoist
Languid horrors
　we all have seen
Finding terror
in loves misery

-pewter, skull, terror

c. churchill

Skin bled dry

of maroon and fire

Passionate plays left us dire

We had too much

of lust to drink

Forever hungover

on loves intoxicating greed

-maroon, skin, passionate

color body feels

I will always remember you

tan skin

lake water welled against our lips

long kiss

skinny dip

losing sun

we created such magic

Sun kissed with summer

We had it all

-tan

c. churchill

color body feels

August

c. churchill

August

1. Scarlet
2. Pinky
3. Revenge
4. Blood
5. Collarbone
6. Happy
7. Goldenrod
8. Teeth
9. Poetic
10. Olive
11. Belly
12. Thankful
13. Lemon
14. Beard
15. Daring
16. Pine
17. Birthday
18. Shattered
19. Teal
20. Nails
21. Alienated
22. Navy
23. Sole
24. Fascinated
25. Melon
26. Freckle
27. Anxious
28. Sepia
29. Smile
30. Loved
31. Grass

color body feels

Her name was Scarlet and she pinky swore

never to kiss him

never to whore

But alas she did

It was not her fault

Revenge lived in a well

Deep inside her heart

She told me she loved him

Before we ever we met

I suppose I was the whore

who left things unsaid

-scarlet, pinky, revenge

c. churchill

The blood rises high upon my
flesh

Burning my collarbone straight
to my neck

Butterflies traveled as they do
up my happiness

Finding the end in you

-blood, collarbone, happy

color body feels

Listless lies couldn't break

A goldenrod smile of everything fake

You took and took until I was dry

Leaving poetic

Leaving me high

-goldenrod, teeth, poetic

c. churchill

If your belly is full

be thankful

Whether it olives and fish

or wine and cheese

A fullness of life

Is one to not grieve

-olive, belly, thankful

color body feels

You were daring yet sweet

A lemon scented beard

And a smile for weeks

I couldn't help it

When you were near

Those are the days

My heart would fear

-lemon, beard, daring

c. churchill

Shattered pieces lay scatter
smiling

Among the pines a birthday
comes

The world infused with magic
creates a destiny

not bought nor sold

just is as is

-pine, birthday, shattered

color body feels

Like nails on a chalkboard you made me scream

As if the world was no longer to be seen

I felt alienated from those who missed out on sweet love

We colored the sky teal above

We came and came falling into ecstasy

Soon we only knew loves brevity

-teal, nails, alienated

c. churchill

I dropped a shoe off the Navy pier

They told me a wish would come this year

The sole floated up not ready to sink

I guess the wishes weren't ready

For a walk in my shoes

-navy, *sole, fascinated*

color body feels

Melons ripe in this sweet season

Freckles primed and laced with treason

Summer beauty is to behold

Anxious smiles full and bold

We live wild on dusk delight

Sneaking every lick

Savoring every bite

-melon, freckle, anxious

c. churchill

The photo sat on the mantle with ease

A hundred years of dust did please

We were vintage lost in memories found

Smiles placed on loved ones crown

We had a legacy to uphold

Within the realm of all things sepia

But always trimmed in gold

-sepia, smile, loved

color body feels

Lay with me in the sweet grass dew

Let me swoon naked plans

Where we dream of clouds and futures high

Laying under a summer sky

-grass

c. churchill

color body feels

September

c. churchill

September

1.	Vanilla
2.	Organ
3.	Blushing
4.	Slate
5.	Chest
6.	Delicate
7.	Onyx
8.	Cell
9.	Glaring
10.	Silver
11.	Brain
12.	Petrified
13.	Jasper
14.	Wings
15.	Fiery
16.	Sand
17.	Gut
18.	Whimsical
19.	Twilight
20.	Bone
21.	Rapture
22.	Lava
23.	Fangs
24.	Wise
25.	Shadow
26.	Pelvis
27.	Vulnerable
28.	Cinnamon
29.	Tear
30.	Satisfied

color body feels

I wasn't young

I was no longer school girl

I had vanilla love mastered

 in all the right ways

But you came hard

Organs blushing

Made me falter

Like a freshman rushing

-vanilla, organ, blushing

c. churchill

Why do we lay our hearts
delicate when our chests heave
till we drop?

Where we would sooner see the
slate sky instead of the
rainbow beneath our pages

Full on loves false promises we
are gaining vigor in a life of
grays

-slate, chest, delicate

color body feels

Oh those eyes filled with onyx
Black as death glaring through
Watching from behind the bars
Of a cell created by you

An inmate of torment
You reside
Behind those bars
Behind your pride

-onyx, cell, glaring

c. churchill

An ounce of silver lets loose the pain

Opium has filled this brain

When we stop, we have petrified

Laced in midnight

Laced in lies

-silver, brain, petrified

color body feels

On blades of Jasper

The mockingbird sings

Wings spread across

A blood let swing

A knife so bold

It comes to lunge

Into a fiery heart

I succumb

-jasper, wings, fiery

c. churchill

Sands of time rob my sleep

Gut wrenching cries

fill me deep

Where does the whimsical grow?

In a place so barren

without my soul

-sand, gut, whimsical

color body feels

Some may fear the rapture
befallen

I myself enjoy this notion

When twilight seeks a
correspondent

I am there in night all calling

My bones have dealt in devil
ways

I cannot assume you would want
to play

-twilight, bone, rapture

c. churchill

I sank them in your veins so deep

I wonder if you were mine to keep

Hot lava poison filled and ready

Word to the wise

My fangs have never been unsteadied

-lava, fangs, wise

color body feels

Color me vulnerable

As your pelvis seeks

A shadow to call home

A heart to keep

Paint love on so thick

For lust is a dirty trick

-shadow, pelvis, vulnerable

c. churchill

Every tear burning hot
Like cinnamon on fresh snow

Was he satisfied?

Not till she was a smolder
That no one could extinguish

-cinnamon, tear, satisfied

color body feels

c. churchill

color body feels

October

c. churchill

October

1. Smoke
2. Ghost
3. Zombie
4. Black cat
5. Mask
6. Celestial
7. Pumpkin
8. Mummy
9. Eerie
10. Mist
11. Costume
12. Howl
13. Moon
14. Corpse
15. Gore
16. Night
17. Spirit
18. Spooky
19. Brimstone
20. Vampire
21. Enchant
22. Decay
23. Wolf
24. Wicked
25. Glow
26. Wizard
27. Scream
28. Shiver
29. Decapitate
30. Dead
31. Treat

color body feels

Curls
In out
Above
Surround

Every bit a habit
Ghosts rarely seen with
Smoke packs deep

Zombies some say
As they shuffle through
Numb with validation

Veins filled
Lungs grieving

Pressing addiction
Slaves of nicotine

-smoke, ghost, zombie

c. churchill

Hide your superstition
From someone who hasn't
seen hell

Black cats cross every
path

They tuck me in at night

Clawing masks of those
who pass

These celestial musings
weren't meant for
naysayer's gasps

-blackcat, mask, celestial

color body feels

Wrap me in linens
Those of mummy kings
Lay me down to sleep

The sky speaks in eerie
psalms
While the grounds turn
pumpkin
Under deaths last sun

Keep me here in a
dreamlike state
For my desert soul is
empty from fate

-pumpkin, mummy, eerie

c. churchill

I wear the sheep as
costume reeking

Into the mist
Prey still sleeping

They stink of blood and
stolen youth

Full bellies engorged
Wealth abused

Making moves of stealth
Answers my empty growl

Realizing soon enough
You can't control deaths
howl

-mist, costume, howl

color body feels

Lay them out
Fresh and still

Life now corpse
Under a moon full

There is no gore
Only peace this night

For they wished
They pleaded

A silent plight

-moon, corpse, gore

c. churchill

Spirits come as night
grows thick

Tapping lightly that's
their trick

Rousing sleep of those
who breathe

A spooky way to make them
believe

-night, spirit, spooky

color body feels

He didn't smell of
brimstone nor death
Rather he was enchanting
Bloodless eyes scanning
the room
I should have known

But still
I was enticed
As he drained my heart
I stole his glance

Leaving neither vampire
nor prey a chance

*-brimstone, vampire,
enchant*

c. churchill

Wicked ways
Wicked plays

I was moon
You were wolf

Heartbeat
Fresh on your lips
Still pulsing

Swallowed whole
No time for decay

As you howled for me
I welcomed your display

-decay, wolf, wicked

color body feels

He wasn't a wizard
Although his magic
Made me scream
Not in fear
But a dangerous glow
One found in love

That one we all know

-glow, wizard, scream

c. churchill

I shiver
I warm
I am not dead

But there is no
connection left

Between body and head
Am I decapitated in
spirit

Or just daydreaming
again?

-shiver, decapitate, dead

color body feels

I was never accepting of
things they called treats
They were somehow always
filled with a sweet
demise
Laced in passive
aggressive
Centers chewing lies
Cotton candy
Razor blades
A stocking full of coal

A life less gifted
A love less soul

-treat

c. churchill

color body feels

November

c. churchill

November

1. Sky
2. Curve
3. Sin
4. Wine
5. Flesh
6. Virtue
7. Ink
8. Sight
9. Anguish
10. Watercolor
11. Swollen
12. Overwhelmed
13. Pear
14. bruised
15. Stoic
16. Cream
17. Flushed
18. Drained
19. Chestnut
20. Braid
21. Pleasant
22. Meadow
23. Forearm
24. Striped
25. Avocado
26. Kiss
27. Naked
28. Cobalt
29. Bleed
30. Frail

color body feels

Touch me bare

Dripping sin

Curve my hand

Round your thigh

Let's create a whirlwind love

Breaking day

Shattering sky

-sky, curve, sin

c. churchill

I held virtue

Like a glass of fine wine

Above my flesh

Behind my mind

A kiss to crack

A vessel deep

Drunk on poetry and promises of keep

-wine, flesh, virtue

color body feels

Second sight

Inked to write

Feels you see

Anguish I bleed

A life of trials

Pen and paper

All the love

Stolen by reaper

Island of one

The widow shore

Debt be paid

I won't borrow any more

-ink, sight, anguish

c. churchill

How could a sky drip

Watercolor ways

Catch a cloud

Swollen

Tipping over

Overwhelmed rains

No matter the bleed

Those tears still come

The sky will weep

-watercolor, swollen,
overwhelmed

color body feels

Center of the table

A bruised pear

A stoic scene

Of what could be

Still life

Is it?

-pear, bruised, stoic

c. churchill

Kitten to cream

A young girls dream

Flushed in pink

Gathering flies

Shit you say to get them high

So full now

Drained only by your

good bye

-cream, flushed, drained

color body feels

Chestnut braids

A full heart

Longing

A girl next door smile

Pleasant she was

This girl you knew

Before you tore her heart
 in two

-chestnut, braids, pleasant

c. churchill

Laying forearm to forearm

Freshly adorned in sin

The sky now larger

Than before we began

Stripped of inhibition

In a meadow of trust

Long grasses soothe

Dew wished this touch

Unsure of anything

We lay silent

In love-soaked lust

-meadow, forearm, stripped

color body feels

Canopy of leaves

A certain sheen

Avocado or was it pale green?

A first kiss sweet

Everything divine

Remember it all

We will be fine

The scent of summer

Naked in thought

Attempting virtue

On promiscuities previous lot

-avocado, kiss, naked

c. churchill

There is a certain chill

That bleeds from the frail

Once a rose cheek

Cobalt now

As the depths

Oceans of waves

Breaking the last shatter

Do you see her

Washed away

-cobalt, bleed, frail

color body feels

c. churchill

color body feels

December

c. churchill

December

1. Ice
2. Arch
3. Frozen
4. Ginger
5. Stride
6. Decadent
7. Cranberry
8. Lift
9. Jubilant
10. Persimmon
11. Tresses
12. Scarce
13. Nutmeg
14. Contort
15. Luscious
16. Eggnog
17. Bite
18. Festive
19. Snowflake
20. Linger
21. Frolic
22. Fire
23. Dance
24. Intoxicated
25. Mistletoe
26. Stretch
27. Joy
28. Glitter
29. Embrace
30. Magical
31. Celebrate

color body feels

I arch my back arms high

Skating on the frozen lake

Winter brings a cool mix

Darkness and white

Beautiful silence

Before the ice boom

Brings me to my knees

I remember

Flashes my vision

Blurred in tears

Screaming. "Daddy no"

As the lake

Swallowed life whole

Winter remains

Darkness covered in white

-ice, arch, frozen

c. churchill

Walking beneath the strides of decadent

Just above ginger roots in soda cans

Jim Beam in bottles

No ice necessary

When the glass

Fills freely

A smile a wink

Another drink

But never quite decadent

-ginger, stride, decadent

color body feels

Cranberries simmer

Lifting high

A past canned jelly

Turkey dry

No longer my life

Holidays move to jubilant

Trimmed in all the bows

The past hidden

in the now rare low

-cranberry, lift, jubilant

c. churchill

I dream of persimmon skies

Lay my tresses wide

A sea of thought

Coursing veins

Hearts that beat

Instead of explain

Dreams run high

Reality scarce

When seas turn to oceans

I scream to dream

Instead I wake

-persimmon, tresses, scarce

color body feels

We were flying that kite

Up so high

Watching from licked lips

Luscious dream

Contorted visions

A nutmeg high

We fly

We dance

We crash

The spices of life

 tasting different

-nutmeg, contort, luscious

c. churchill

Drink the potion
Bite the illusion

Swallowed in festive confusion
Eggnog drips
 from mouths of babes

While parents scream
Laughing cascades
The holiday tree
a flame in the corner

Never knowing life exists
Beyond brick or mortar

-eggnog, bite, festive

color body feels

I love the linger
　of winters song
Silent storms
　where snowflakes frolic
Among the trees
　we find our warm
In the hands
　another year worn

-snowflake, linger, frolic

c. churchill

The fire has been a faithful light

Always dancing while I write

Embers glow in sweet warming

Winters night keeps on growing

I choose to tell

a long-intoxicated tale

For those who have stayed

From dusk till morning

-fire, dance, intoxicated

color body feels

I found joy in

Your hand

Small back

Pulled close

Mistletoe

Stretched to kiss

Things normal people know

Things I hold as miracles

-mistletoe, stretch, joy

c. churchill

You took my fear

Embraced me

Till the dark pools

Turned to glitter

Settling like a snowfall

Maybe when things are magical

It just means they are finally right

-glitter, embrace, magical

color body feels

Have you been to the place

The one where procrastination eats away at your soul

Where the day is more frightening than the night

Where effort seems futile

You are not alone

I have been there

I lived there far too long

Write it out

Leave it on tear stained pages

Fill the spaces with

New life, new love

New words.

-celebrate

c. churchill

About the author:

Cheryl Churchill is a writer and artist from a small town in Michigan. She has been writing and creating art most of her life. She is currently pursuing a master's degree from the University of Michigan.

She has lived all over the United States and actively travels to see as much of the world as she can. Some may say she is a nomad, but she is just filled with wanderlust.

In her debut poetry collection, I am a woman Not a Winston, she has included her beautiful photography. The photography in this book was done by her as well.

You can find her on IG: @cc_writes

On FB: facebook.com/cchurchillwrites

c. churchill

Keep writing

Write from the heart

Keep writing

So much love to all my support
team in the writing community.

I feel blessed every day to
know such incredible people.

Thank you for the continued
support.

        Love to you,

                Cheryl

color body feels

Made in the USA
Lexington, KY
07 August 2019